To Imogen,

A B⬤OK ABOUT US

Trusting you will enjoy
reading each story and
feel inspired to write
your own ☺ would
love to read all about
you!

Eliana
Summer 2024

A B🌍OK ABOUT US

Celebrating Diversity

ELI KEEN

Library of Congress Control Number: 2012900030S
ISBN: Hardcover   978-1-4691-4868-7
                 Softcover   978-1-4691-4867-0
                 Ebook   978-1-4691-4869-4

This book was printed in the United States of America.

To order additional copies of this book, contact:
Xlibris Corporation
0-800-644-6988
www.xlibrispublishing.co.uk
Orders@xlibrispublishing.co.uk
303091

CONTENTS

I dedicate this book to my son Kern and to every single child across and around our beautiful planet Earth. I also dedicate it to the inner child that eternally lives in ALL of us deserving and worthy of the love, care and attention that we are meant to get.

In mind and spirit,

Eli Keen

Cowbridge, Wales – UK

Spring 2012

Be Talk™ is a series of books for children and young people focused on Self, Cultural and Social Awareness with a view to promote personal development and collective growth.

If there is **light** in the **heart**, there is love in the person.

If there is **love** in the **person**, there is harmony in the home.

If there is **harmony** in the home, there is order in the nation.

And if there is **order** in the **nation**, there is **Peace on Earth**

(A Chinese proverb)

Volume one: *The United Kingdom of Great Britain and Northern Ireland.*

This volume is the first step towards a long journey around the globe where English is spoken in Schools as an official language. An invitation to know more about our lives told by different children and young people around the globe.

In this volume, you will get to 'meet' Rhys from Wales, Sheena from Northern Ireland, Stuart from Scotland, and Vicki Benbow from England who will, in future volumes, travel and meet children from all over the world.

Introduction

Hello! My name is Eliana Keen and before I talk of this book, I would like to tell you just a little bit about myself. I was born in Brazil in 1962. I came to live in Wales in 1989 married to a Welshman named Roger. I am a school counsellor, teacher, and workshop leader. My most important role, however, is being a mother. I have a teenage son called Kern, who has been the greatest source of inspiration and strength for me.

My work with children and young people is very precious to me. It is the reason why I have written this book and to offer you the opportunity to learn more about yourself, the relationship we have with each other, and the beautiful planet we share and care for.

A *Book About Us* is the first volume in the series and features four stories of four British children—one from each country that makes up the United Kingdom.

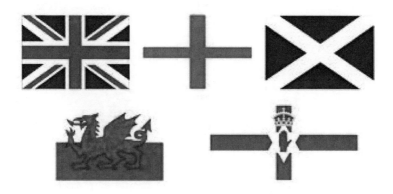

Our Welsh boy, Rhys, lives in the rural market town of Cowbridge in the Vale of Glamorgan. Sheena is from Northern Ireland and lives in Portaferry, County Down. Stuart is a young Scotsman, who absolutely loves fishing and comes from Kelty. And our English young lady, Vicki from Chingford near London, will take us on a colourful journey meeting children from all corners of our beautiful and diverse planet earth.

As you know, the United Kingdom is made up of four distinct and unique countries—Wales, Northern Ireland, Scotland, and England. The British Isles are situated in the North Western coast of Europe between the North Sea and the Atlantic Ocean. Our young friends Rhys, Sheena, Stuart, and Vicki will tell their personal stories and tell us a little bit about the places where they live and how they like living there.

Well, that's enough from me. Let me introduce you to Rhys Davies. He is going to talk about himself and his family life. I wonder how many of you will have some things in common with him. Anyway, I hope you will enjoy this first book in the series during our adventure in search of finding out All About Us!

WALES

Ħi! Ϻy name is Ꞧhys Ɖavies. Ɉ was born at the Princess of Wales Ħospital in Bridgend, a town in South Wales. Ɉ am ten years old and live with my mum, Leah, and our cat Ϻax in Cowbridge. When Ɉ was born, Ɉ lived in another place called *Bryncethin* near Bridgend, with my mum and dad. Ϻy parents split up when Ɉ was three and then my mum and Ɉ moved to Cowbridge. Ϻy dad moved to London, in England and Ɉ go to stay with him during school holidays. Ħe used to come and pick me up, and we travelled by train, which was great fun. Now he comes in his car, and I like that as well.

I don't really mind that my parents are not together. They used to argue before they split up so now it feels more relaxed with just one of them around me. In fact, I quite like it because I can have them all to myself—☺

I go to *Y Bont Faen* Primary School, and I'm in year six. My class teacher is called Ms Jones, and she is quite cool and a good teacher. My favourite subject is PE as I am mad about football. I support Manchester United, and I would love to become a football player. I play football with my friends all the time and play for the Cowbridge Juniors team. I would really love to become a professional footballer. The national game in Wales is rugby but I prefer playing football. I play it with my friends after school and at weekends. We go to this place called 'Astro Turf' by the local leisure centre. It's a great place.

Well, let me talk a bit about my family.. My mother is very kind and patient with me. She is a great cook, and I love her food. She always listens to music when she is cooking. My mum is so funny. She dances around the house when she is cleaning and playing her CD's. It's also funny when she speaks to our cat Max. My mum goes to college at the moment. She wants to go back to work when I go to Cowbridge Comprehensive School next year. I'm looking forward to going to comprehensive school so I can meet some of my friends I went to school with at St. David's school in Colwinston before I came to *Y Bont Faen. My best friend at school at the moment is Harry. It is a shame Harry doesn't play football with me but we play X-box and he is really funny and clever. I call on him on my way to school every morning and we chat on the way there. It's nice to have friends we can talk to. Harry's mum and dad are separated as well but he has two older brothers. Sometimes I wonder what it would be like to have a brother or a sister . . .*

Y Bont Faen means Cowbridge in Welsh. We learn Welsh in school, but our main language is English. We do have another school in Cowbridge and the teachers and pupils there speak and teach in Welsh. English and Welsh are the two languages spoken in Wales. My class teacher taught us that the reason why we speak English is because Wales was invaded by the Normans and then conquered by the English who changed the law of the time. It's okay though. I think it is different—and good—to learn two languages. Wales, in welsh is *Cymru. I love the red dragon on our Welsh flag. And I like being Welsh because it is more than being British. It feels special.*

Cowbridge is a small town and I like it because my mum lets me go out and play with my friends. I can walk to school, and I feel safe. It's not too busy and noisy like Cardiff, London, and other big cities. Cardiff is the capital of Wales. I like going to Cardiff ice skating at the Winter Wonderland we have every year around Christmas time. I love the snow at Christmas. I think it is magic. My mum loves it too and when it snows, if it is safe to drive, we go for a drive near the mountains called Brecon Beacons. There is a National Park there and it is a cool place.

Did you know that the highest mountain in the world was named after a Welshman called Sir George Everest? Mount Everest is in Nepal and is part of the Himalayan mountain range.

Anyway, in the spring and summer when the weather is nice I love going to Llantwit Major, a town in the sea side near Cowbridge. On some weekends, my mum gets some chips for us, and we eat it on the beach after school. I love looking for crabs in the rock pools. On the way back home, we always stop at the Rainbow Plaza to get a DVD and some treats so we can relax and have some fun together.

I love it when mum and I go to the pictures as well and have a pizza at Pizza Hut. We like going to McArthur Glen shopping centre near Bridgend and sometimes my mum drives past the house we used to live. I remember my bedroom there. It was very colourful with balloons, stars, and a moon that dad painted on the wall. I have photos of it, and that helps me remember.

Talking of my dad, most half-terms, he comes to pick me up and takes me to his flat in London. I like it when I go to stay with my dad. He always takes me out to get some new clothes and takes me for a haircut too. He also buys me lots of sweets. My dad is great. His name is Charles, and he works really hard because he has to work during the night. He is a printer, and he told me the machines need to work all night long to print newspapers, magazines, etc. I don't understand this very well, but I know he gets really tired. Then he has to sleep during the day. Sounds a bit weird. Imagine having to stay up all night then sleep in the day time? How about in the summer time when it's so nice and sunny outside, and you have to go to bed? Poor dad. I wish he didn't have to work so hard. But he said it's okay. He got used to it, and when I go and stay with him, he has time off and we play fights, watch the telly, and play X-box together.

As I told you, I love football, but when I am not playing football, I like watching television. I also like playing FIFA on my Play Station 2. I'm an only child, and sometimes I get a bit bored playing on my own, so I go to one of my friend's house or he comes to mine. I like inviting a friend to stay for a sleepover on the weekends sometimes. It's great when my mum makes homemade pizza so we can roll our own pizza and put the toppings we like. I don't like cheese, so I put on lots of bacon, mushroom, peppers, and sweet corn. I love pizza. It's also fun because my friend and I get to sleep downstairs on the sofa bed, and we can watch a bit of telly until mum says it's time to go to sleep.

Talking of food, my favourite food in the whole world is a roast dinner—especially lamb. I love lamb with roast potatoes and minty gravy. Both my mum and my dad love cooking. When I go to my dad's house, he buys a huge leg of lamb for us. This is making me hungry . . . in fact, I could eat a roast dinner right now!

I live in a terraced house in a row of seven houses. I like my house. It's small, but we have all we need. The only thing I do wish we had in our house was a bigger garden so I could play more football. Our garden is quite small. And it has a pond and a few flower beds so there isn't much space for me to play and my mum would get upset if I damaged any flowers. My mum doesn't work at the moment because she looks after me and goes to college. She said she is investing in a new career or something.

Winter 2010. We had lots of snow!

This is the street where I live on the other side of the high street so it's not too far to go and buy sweets ☺

Anyway, I think I have said enough about me. Ms Keen, the teacher who asked my mum if I would write about myself said that she is going to make this into a book and that there will be other kids telling their stories. She said that one of the kids in this book is going to travel and meet children from other countries. I wish I get to be the kid who gets to travel. I love travelling. I guess I would anyway. If this book is going to travel, then my story will travel with it. Well, it's been fun doing this, and it would be nice to hear you tell your story too. I hope you enjoy the photos and the bits about Cowbridge. It is a small and friendly town. We have lots of fairs and festivals, but my favourite one is the Christmas reindeer parade. Hope you can come and visit one day. Hwyl Fawr! That's 'goodbye' in Welsh.

This is the high street where the town hall and all the shops are. The building on the picture is the town hall. We have a community group called

Big Screen, and they show films there every month. They also have fairs and sometimes concerts and talks and choirs.

Cowbridge Town Hall at Christmas 2010.

Teaching Tools: Insert One

Now it is your turn to introduce yourself, the people in your life, the places you go to and the place you live in. You will create your own book and tell your own story.

Your teacher will assist you with some prompting questions if you need or you can choose to write freely.

ALL About Me

NORTHERN IRELAND

Hello, I'm Sheena Kelly, and I am eleven years old. I was born in Belfast, the capital of Northern Ireland, but I live in Portaferry, County Down with my parents. My mum is expecting a baby, and I am really excited about having a baby brother or sister. I really don't mind if it's a boy or a girl I just want him or her to arrive soon.

I love helping my mum around the house so I think I will love helping her with the baby—but I hope he or she won't cry all the time. My grandma told me that small babies cry a lot. Well, I suppose if you can't talk and don't know how to say what you need, then crying seems the only way you get heard. Anyway, let me talk a little bit about me. Ms Keen is this special teacher who came to our school to talk to us about **emotional intelligence**. She asked us if anyone was interested in writing about their lives and then have their stories published in a book. Well, I love reading, so I thought I would have a go at writing too.

So here it goes. I go to St. Patrick's Primary school, where I have a few friends. My best friend is my next-door neighbour, Robin. She is two years older than me and goes to Saintfield high school. We used to go to school together, but now we can only see each other after school and at weekends. She says she misses primary school and that life at Saintfield High is very different from St. Patrick's.

I love music, and I am learning how to play the piano. My mother loves music too, and she is very artistic. We do lots of arts and crafts together, and we always have great fun. I wonder if we will still have time to do these things when the baby comes. I imagine babies need a lot of attention.

My dad is a journalist and works for a big newspaper in Belfast, so he is away a lot. He is always travelling abroad as well, so I don't get to see him very much. Often, when he comes home from work or from his travels, I am already in bed and then when I go to school, he is still asleep. I would love to visit some of the places he has been to. He always brings us gifts from all over the world. I have dolls from China, Russia, and other places I can't even spell or remember.

I don't know what I want to do when I grow up yet, but I do like music, and I absolutely love books. I read all of the time. My favourite author is J. K. Rowling as I love the magical world of Harry Potter. I would love to write books or poems. Maybe I will compose music or write scripts for films or television. When I come home from school, I usually have to go to the library to return and to borrow some more books, or I go to my piano lessons. I also go to ballet classes, but I am not too keen on classical dance. Maybe, I would like doing jazz or even tap dancing as I'm very bouncy.

I like spending time reading and daydreaming. I love fantasising and pretending I am one of the characters I am reading about. It's great fun because in your head you can go anywhere you like. My grandma Dorothy sometimes says I look as if I have my head in the clouds.

Grandma is a very wise woman. She has read a lot of books in her lifetime and has learned a lot from them, so she always has something clever to say. She is mummy's mother. Granddad is dead now. I don't remember him, but I like looking at the photo albums we have in our house. I was very little when he died. Mummy told me he had a heart problem. I wonder what happens to you when you die. Mummy and I talk about these things. I love listening to grandma talking about the part of us that never dies—our soul. Some people call it spirit. I'm not sure if there is a difference between soul and spirit. How about our thoughts? Where do they come from? Could that be what the soul does? Helps us think, feel, and be in the world? I have a lot of questions in my head. That's why I like it when Grandma comes because I know she sits down with a cup of tea with mummy and they will talk about how things have been and all that. Grandma comes every week and sometimes on some Sundays as well to have lunch with us when dad is away.

I spend a lot of time in my room, especially when it is so dark and cold outside during the winter months. I don't like going out when it's cold, and I don't like the wind very much either. I like staying indoors, though. It's cosy and warm. My mum bakes a lot of cakes and bread. I love the smell of baking. She makes lots of cupcakes with decorations on top. I help her sometimes, and I'm sure I'll be able to make them on my own as well, but it's so much more fun doing it together. 'I love you mummy!' Mummy and I are very close. I love feeling the baby moving in her tummy. It feels really weird to think there is a baby inside mummy's tummy and that soon he or she will come out and live with us. I can't wait! ☺

We live in a three-bedroom house on Oliver Close in Ballygalget, Portaferry. I like living there. Robin lives at number 6, and we spend time together at the weekend. We listen to music in my room and talk. Robin plays the piano as well, and we like practicing together. We help each other out.

Sometimes we do our homework together too, and she helps me if I get stuck.

Portaferry is lovely. We have a marina, and I love it when my dad is home at weekends as he takes us there for a treat. We have lunch in a restaurant then go for a walk or watch the boats. We have the coolest aquarium in town as well. It is amazing to see all the different kinds of fish. I copied some photos for you, but if you want to see more, you can go on the Internet and google Portaferry Marina or Portaferry Aquarium.

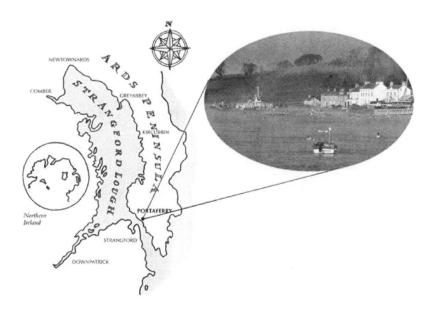

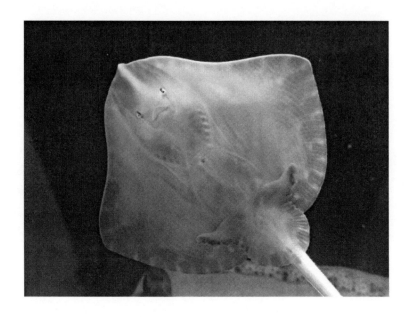

Portaferry Aquarium

Northern Ireland is the smallest part of the United Kingdom. Northern Ireland was once part of Ireland however. I learned in school that in 1801 the whole of Ireland became part of the United Kingdom but after many years of civil war—that's when there is a conflict between groups of citizens, the people of the same country, fighting for different things. Some of the people wanted to be indendpendent so Britain made a deal with Ireland to keep the six counties in the north-east of Ireland. These six counties now make up what is known as Northern Ireland. The southern part of the island is the Republic of Ireland, or Eire. In 1927—The current name of the UK, the **United Kingdom of Great Britain and Northern Ireland,** was chosen.

I love History and Geography and I find it is important to know about things that made the country I live in today. It's also interesting to know about special people and things that has to do with the Country we are born in.

Did you know that the ship Titanic was built in Belfast? The Titanic was a passenger liner that hit an iceberg on her very first trip from England to New York City, and sank on 15 April 1912. It must have been so scary for the passengers . . .

And did you know that C.S. Lewis, a legend writer, was born in Belfast as well? I adore his books and the Narnia series are absolutely brilliant! So what's special about the Country you come from?

I think it is fascinating that we have unique things about ourselves and the places we come from. We are all special for being different and I don't understand when people fight or don't like each other because they are different. I think being different makes us richer and more beautiful, don't you?

I hope you have enjoyed getting to know a little bit about me. Ms Keen told me that she intends to create a blog or a website to give every child and young people the chance to talk about things that affect us like school work and home life. I think it's a really good idea to have a safe place where we can just talk about what it's going on in our heads and in our hearts. With Ms Keen and other teachers like her, we can understand our emotions and feelings a little better. She said it's very important to be in touch with how we feel and learn to express ourselves in a way that doesn't upset anybody. People don't like anyone being nasty or mean to them, do they? But some people can be really mean, and I don't get it.

Sometimes, when mummy and daddy are unhappy and argue with each other, I feel confused. I talk to mummy afterwards, but she doesn't always have the answers. Maybe, she gets confused too. People like Ms Keen can help us, and I am very glad that she cares so much. When she came to my school to work with us and talked to us about emotional intelligence, I learned a lot about myself. I had only heard about being intelligent as in 'being clever'. Ms Keen talked to us about how important it is for us to know how to deal with our feelings so that they don't hurt us or anyone else.

I'm very excited to write about myself. Ms Keen said that one of the children in her books will travel to meet other schoolchildren from countries where they speak English as well like America, Australia, Canada, South Africa, and even Nepal!

Okay, I talk a lot. I never realised that before really although mummy is always saying that I never stop talking. I think she is right ☺ How about you? Do you talk a lot? If you do, maybe we can talk online someday. So until then, goodbye for now!

Teaching Tools: Insert Two

Hey guys! How are you? Are you enjoying writing about yourself? Did you enjoy reading about Sheena? It must be exciting to be expecting a baby to arrive in your life, don't you think? I wonder if there might be any of you going through or have gone through this experience.

I was the youngest in my family, so I missed out on that one. But obviously, I had the experience of becoming a mother which has been—and still is—the most amazing experience. A real blessing and such a responsibility. I hope Sheena's baby brother or sister will bring her and her family much joy. Babies need a lot of care and attention, don't they? They arrive with a huge presence and takes centre stage for quite some time. Babies grow into toddlers and become more independent. Babies learn very quickly and are very present in how they live and experience the outside world.

When I say outside world, I say that in reference to our inner world. As you know, we have a body, a mind, and a spirit through our being present in the world, we get to experience who we are. So far, you have written certain facts about yourself. In the next session of the story you will be invited to think about what you think about. In other words, I will ask you some questions about the way you think about certain things. You may well start expressing how you feel about it too. We must connect the body, the mind, and the spirit in order to have a full and meaningful experience in life. I trust you will find this useful and interesting.

ALL About Me

SCOTLAND

My name is Stuart McGregor, and I am almost eleven years old. My birthday is in just three weeks' time, and I am very excited about it because my dad is taking me fishing to Loch Leven. I love fishing. My dad has a boat, and he has been taking me fishing with him since I was very little.

I live in Kelty, Fife in Scotland with my mom Aileen, my two half-sisters, and my step-dad. Jessie is five and Kelya is only two. They are both very funny, and I love them very much.

I'm the big brother, and I like playing with them. Kelya makes me laugh so much with her funny way of talking gibberish.

My mom and dad got divorced when I was about two, then my mother got married to Graham and my dad married Brenda. I also have a step-brother. His name is Connor, and he is seven years old. He will be going fishing with us next month. We are camping. Just the boys, though, as my step-mom hates camping and can't stand fishing. I absolutely love being outdoors. It can be very cold in Scotland, but I don't mind. My dad always says, 'There is no such thing as bad weather—only bad clothing.' You have to have good clothing in Scotland. Besides, I'm used to it. My dad is called Callum. He is a fisherman—in case you haven't guessed!

Anyway, I go to Kelty Primary, and in September, I'll go to Lochgelly High School. I like my school, but I don't have many friends there. My best friend, Brian, moved to Australia last year. I miss him a lot. We keep in touch on the Internet, but it's not the same because we can't walk to school together and play with each other anymore. He is coming over for a holiday next year to visit his Nan and other relatives and my dad said that when I turn sixteen and if I do well in my GCSE exams, I can go to Australia for a month. Wow, can you imagine that? Brian said it's very different from Scotland and that people there find it very hard to understand his English. Well, I've heard a lot of people find it difficult to understand the way we talk.

I miss Brian. I wonder what it's like to live in Australia. I love Scotland, but it would be fun to be able to go and live in different places as well. See different things and meet different people. I have decided I am going to work hard at school and get good GCSE results so my dad sends me to spend a month with my friend Brian. He is quite excited about it as well as we both talk about making plans and keeping in touch with each other.

I don't have many friends in school. I am quite shy and don't really go out of my way to talk to others and play with them. I spend more of my time reading or just looking around, looking at my friends playing and running around. Some of them tease me because I'm so quiet. But that's okay, I'm used to it now, and I try not to let it bother me. I can talk about it with my mom. She understands me and says that I am right in being the way I feel comfortable 'in my own skin' she says. She said we don't have to do what other people want us to do. Some people even dare you to do things that you know isn't right or can even be dangerous for us. Like once this boy in school dared me to walk on the thin ice in the beginning of last winter. Mad, isn't it? Why would I want to do that? Then he called me a 'scaredy cat'. I didn't bother me because I did what I felt it was right and didn't feel pressured into doing something just to show off. My dad always talks to me about those things and warns me about peer pressure. He said it can be tough when you get to a certain age and other boys are starting to experiment with things like alcohol and drugs and pressure you to do it too. Better not to get involved, right?

Anyway, that's why I miss my friend Brian. He is like me in many ways. We both like reading and exploring nature—camping, fishing, and walking on different paths and trails. We both like writing on a scrap book and decorating it with stuff we draw or stick on like leaves and interesting things we find. We always take our scrap books and do some nature drawing. We learned some tricks in school, and it is good to have a go. Me and Brain used to have some competitions between ourselves then take to our Art teacher Mr Murray to choose the best one.

Now that Brian moved, I spend more time with my mom helping with the girls. Mom works at the local school a few days a week. She helps some pupils who find it hard to learn things. I think everything in school happens very quickly. I wish we had more time to talk about the things we are learning to help us to understand them better. I do try hard to keep up with all that we are told to do. Year six has been totally mad. And to think I'm going to the 'big school' in September, it freaks me out a little bit. There will be so much more to learn and to do. I have to keep up if I want those grades and my ticket to a holiday with Brian. I'm very lucky that I have my mom and that she is able to help me. My mom is a Learning Support Assistant and I think she is very good at her job. She is very patient and doesn't shout like some teachers do. I don't like it when teachers shout. But it must be very difficult to be a teacher I think. Some classmates can be a real pain and keep disturbing the class so the teacher sometimes loses patience, I suppose.

I love being a Scotsman. Have you ever heard of Hogmanay? It is the Scottish name for New year's Eve and the children can go round different houses asking for presents. It's great fun as family, friends and neighbours get together to celebrate the start of a new year by dancing and eating special foods all night long.

I have to go now because my mom needs me to play with little Kels whilst she prepares our dinner. It's been great talking about me with you, and I hope you have enjoyed my story. Of course, there is a lot more I could talk about, so maybe we can get in touch through the Internet. And wherever you are, I hope you enjoy living where you do. Take care! I hope you like the pictures and the bits of information about where I come from. Hope you can visit Scotland one day.

Scotland has many lochs or lakes, and all of them together cover about six hundred miles. The most famous loch is the loch Ness because there is said to be a monster living there, Nessie.

Scotland has about fourteen universities. St. Andrews is one of the oldest founded in 1410 is where Prince William, now the Duke of Cambridge studied.

Edinburgh, the capital, has the many famous theatres and the most famous actor from Scotland is probably Sean Connery.

Lochore Meadows is beautiful countryside. I love walking as well as fishing. There are woodlands, meadows, and grasslands, ponds, a nature reserve, and, of course, Loch Ore. There are paths and trails, and I love being with the trees and our rich environment. The birds and squirrels. I love Scotland!

Kelty, Heritage trail Kelty, Benarty hill

Teaching tools:
Insert three

- What are you thinking about now?

- What kind of things do you think about when you go to sleep?

- Do you think about the day you had?

- Do different things you think about, make you feel different emotions?

- Think of an example.

- Please talk about the best memory you have. How old were you? What is your first memory of yourself?

- What do you think about when you see yourself as a baby in a photograph?

ALL About Me

ENGLAND

Hiya! My name is Vicki and I am English. Before I tell you anything else about me, I'd like to dedicate a poem to you. I wrote this poem one morning based on some dreams I had been having. I dream a lot. Some of my teachers say that I dream even when I am awake. The poem is called: '*In my dreams*' **LOL!**

In my dreams

Flickering flicker of light
Hovers over me throughout the night
Waking my spirit, showing the way.
Free from all burdens that chain my body
And mind each day.

In my dreams, I awake
In my dreams, I can fly
In my dreams, I unlock what is sacred
To release, the divine.

Vicki Benbow

Well, I hope you didn't think it is too weird. I have talked to my mother about my dreams, and what the poem means to me. I'm sure the teacher that will be working with you through our stories will be able to have a discussion with you about what the poem might mean to you. Or even talk about the kind of dreams you have. In my dreams, I could really feel that I was soaring in the sky. It was great fun. A bit scary to start with but then I used to go to bed wishing I could fly in my dreams again. Have you ever had a dream that you really liked? LOL!

Anyway, I'm Vicki. I'm almost eleven. My birthday is on 16th September. I live in Chingford with my mum, dad, two sisters, one brother, one dog, one cat, and a rabbit. It's a busy house. I'm the youngest and the quietest. I don't think that I'm too shy like my brother keeps saying. I just don't feel I have to do what everybody else is doing. I like staying in the kitchen when my mum is cooking so we can talk, and I help her by setting the table or whatever she feels I can do for her. She is always very busy, but somehow, she always manages to give us all some quality time. She says this is extremely important in a healthy relationship. My mum is a counsellor and teacher, and I think she's very clever. I love my mum. I love all my family, but it's more difficult with brothers and sisters who can be mean to us sometimes. It feels like we are competing with each other for attention.

Ms Keen is my personal health and social education PHSE teacher at school, and she asked me to write about myself and the way I live. She said I could speak through my heart by getting in touch with my emotions and feelings. I love writing, so I was really thrilled when she asked me to do this. And then when she said she was going to publish my story in a book, I thought, 'Oh my god, so other school children are going to read about me?' Ms Keen said that culture and the people from each different place in the world makes Earth a very rich and beautiful planet. Her book is called *A Book About Us*. I can't wait to read it. It has the stories of another three children from the United Kingdom. I'd love to meet them personally as I already read their stories. I got inspired and more motivated to write about mine. It's not always easy to talk or write about us from the heart. It feels sometimes that we have to hide our feelings and emotions. So I'm really glad I have Ms Keen as my PHSE teacher in school.

Okay, so here it goes. All about me:

I go to Chingford Church of England Junior School. I do like school, but sometimes, I feel I don't fit in. Sometimes I find it too noisy and everything happens too fast. Too much for us to learn and deal with. As an eleven year old, I feel sometimes I don't get to play and feel free to imagine and contemplate the world that happens in my head and heart. I like going to the loft where it's quiet so I can read my books, write my poems or paint and draw. I love drawing, and I love painting. I love half—terms, so I can have more time to spend in the loft, especially in winter times. I love winters. We had a lot of snow this winter and although it was very beautiful, it did cause a lot of problems. I had never seen so much snow and ice. It was fun for a while, and we couldn't even go to school for a few days as it was dangerous to drive and to walk around.

Mrs Pattison is my class teacher. She said that the planet Earth is going through a climate change and that we needed to look after our environment by recycling and being more careful with how we use energy fuels and things like that. I don't understand how everything works yet, but I think it's important that we understand it better. The Earth is our home, and we have to look after our home and each other.

In my house, because there is so much to do and it's so busy, we all have jobs to do to help my mum and dad. I love feeding my pets. My cat Toulouse, my dog Sissa, and my rabbit Pom-pom. Well, they are not just mine, and we all love them, but it is my job to feed them and make sure their water bowl is clean and has fresh water every day. My dog gets really excited when it's dinner time. She jumps with joy, knowing that she's going to eat. I love eating my food too. I absolutely love Sunday dinners, and it's nice that we are all home and eat together in the dining room. During the week, we eat at the kitchen table and sometimes we don't eat at the same time. My eldest sister Jane is doing her A levels, and she's always in her room studying. She wants to go to university in Italy. She is interested in art and foreign languages. I like other languages too. I always try to learn how to say a few things in the local languages when we go on holiday abroad. We have been to France a few times, and I love speaking a little bit of French. I learn a little bit more each time I go there.

My brother Doug and sister Rita go to Chingford Foundation School. Rita said it's very different from primary school and that it can be a bit scary to begin with. I don't know what I want to do yet, but I do know, I like writing. I love painting too. I get on much better really well with my eldest sister Jane. She is very lucky because she has her own bedroom. I have to share my room with Rita, and sometimes, she can be a bit mean to me. Rita is very messy too. She's always on the phone or on facebook. I love her though. I love everyone in my family.

Well, what else can I say about my life? Oh, I don't think I told you anything about my dad. And by the way, my mum's name is Ana and my dad's name is Arthur. My dad works a lot too. He works in a place like a bank, but not a bank. Dad told me he helps people by making sure their money, houses, cars and other important things are safe and protected with insurance. He is a manager at the company he works for and he works a lot. I think it must be quite hard to work and look after lots of things at the same time. Look after us children and give us everything we need. Take us on holidays and make sure we are cleaning our teeth everyday 😊 My mum is amazing. She went back to work about three years ago. She went to university when I started primary school. She said she used to teach English and Portuguese before. She spent a few years in Brazil, which is in South America, before she met my dad. We've been to Brazil on holidays twice. It's such a big country. I don't remember the first time very well, but when we went there last year, I had a wonderful holiday. We did some cycling and stayed at difference beaches. Beautiful sandy beaches and the weather was perfect. I love travelling and talking of travelling, my school has a link with a school in Nepal, and the head teacher Mrs Nayler is organising a visit to Nepal, and I'm entering in the competition Ms Keen is running to see who goes to this place called Kathmandu, meet some local children, and go to their school for a few days. I really hope I get to go. My parents said that it would be an amazing experience.

I'm sure you know that London is the capital of England and where Queen Elizabeth II—our present day queen lives. The name of her Palace is Buckingham.

England is hugely known and famous all around the world but did you know that in size, it is seventy-four times smaller than the USA, fifty-nine times smaller than Australia, and three times smaller than Japan?

And English, the language from England is spoken in many different countries. I find that quite fascinating and I am looking forward to travelling to some of those places to meet as many different children as possible so they can tell us about themselves and their countries. It is really interesting to think that such a small Country which is in fact, an island, gave the world the English language which is now spoken so widely across the planet. Isn't it fascinating?

Actually, I think the whole world is fascinating and beautiful which makes us **all** fascinating and beautiful too. What do you think? So many different names, faces, voices, colours, customs, festivals, traditions and yet, despite being different on the outside, I think we are pretty the same on the inside. We all have a body with a heart, mind and soul. We all need food, a place to live and people around us to love and feel loved.

Well, there is so much I could tell you about me, but I think I have said a lot already. How about you having a go? It was actually fun to sit down and write about myself and the people around me. In a way, it made me realise how much I love my family, and how important they are to me.

Ms Keen said she will be publishing other children's stories from all over the world. I hope you have enjoyed getting to know a little bit about me, Rhys, Sheena, and Stuart. I know I have. I think it is important for us to share and learn about and from each other. I hope you have fun doing that in your classroom.

But before I go, have a look at some photos of Chingford. We have a forest nearby—Epping Forest, and I love going there in the autumn. It is so beautiful. Sissa, my dog, loves it when we take her in the car and go to the forest for a walk. My mum loves walking there too.

This is the Royal Forest Hotel in the town centre.

This is the bus station.

The Train Station is just next door.

Epping Forest

I hope you have enjoyed my story and the stories of my British neighbours. I also hope that you will have lots of fun writing about yourself, the people in your life and the place where you live. I look forward to sharing the stories of the children I will meet in my travels with Ms Keen in her future books.

Until next time!!!

Teaching tools: Insert four

- What kind of things are important to you?

- Who is your role model?

- What kind of things do you believe about God?

- What is good about the community you live in?

- Write something about your school, your teachers, your school mates, and your daily routine there.

- What is your favourite subject? Why?

- Tell me about your family, your house, and about where you live.

- Where have you been on holidays? Where was your favourite place? Tell me a bit about your experience there.

- What place or places would you like to go one day? What is it about it that attracts you? What do you know about it?

ALL About Me

GLOSSARY

1. The role of a counsellor: A counsellor is a person we can talk to when we feel sad and confused. A counsellor can help us understand our feelings.

2. The role of a learning coach: As part of the 14 to 19 Learning Pathway, the Welsh Assembly government offered training and introduced learning coaches in secondary schools to work with young people in assisting them to aim to achieve their potential by looking at learning as a big picture as part of their 'Learning Country' vision (Turnbull J., 2009)

3. The role of a life coach: A life coach is a trained professional who works with individuals with a view to creating strategies to achieve goals by helping them in their action steps.

4. The role of a learning support assistant: A learning support assistants work directly with pupils who find it more challenging to keep up with

the curriculum and may need extra support in completing tasks and processing information.

5. PSE: Personal and Social Education is the school subject that 'undertakes to support and promote the personal and social development and well-being of its learners' (PSE framework for seven to nineteen year olds in Wales)

6. Emotional intelligence: Emotional intelligence encompasses self-awareness, self-motivation, empathy, social skills, and emotional management. It is highly important to be emotionally intelligent, which is a skill that can be learned.

7. Awareness: An ability of be in tune with what you are experiencing in your body, your mind, and your spirit.

Lightning Source UK Ltd.
Milton Keynes UK
UKOW050512020612

193816UK00001B/14/P